PIECES OF AIR IN THE EPIC

BRENDA HILLMAN

Pieces of Air in the Epic

WESLEYAN UNIVERSITY PRESS

MIDDLETOWN, CONNECTICUT

WESLEYAN POETRY

Published by Wesleyan University Press
Middletown, CT 06459

Copyright © 2005
All rights reserved

Design and composition by Quemadura
Printed in the United States of America
on acid-free, recycled paper

Library of Congress Cataloging-in-Publication Data
Hillman, Brenda.
Pieces of air in the epic / Brenda Hillman.
p. cm. — (Wesleyan poetry)
ISBN 0-8195-6787-6
I. Title. II. Series.
PS3558.I4526P54 2005
811'.54—dc22
2005018749

CONTENTS

ONE

FOR HELEN AND JIMMYE HILLMAN,

AND FOR NANCY LEA BRATT,

FRANCES LERNER, AND NAN NORENE

One

There are long stone looms as well, where the nymphs weave out
their webs from clouds of sea-blue wool . . . The cave has two ways in—

THE ODYSSEY

and she sings: Someone is spinning silk . . .

FRANZ HESSEL

STREET CORNER

There was an angle

where I went for

centuries not as a

self or feature but

exhaled as a knowing

brick tradesmen engineered for

blunt or close recall;

soundly there, meanings grew

past a second terror

finding their way as

evenings, hearing the peppermint

noise of sparrows landing

like spare dreams of

citizens where abstraction and

the real could merge.

We had crossed the

red forest; we had

recognized a weird lodge.

We could have said

song outlasts poetry, words

are breath bricks to

support the guardless singing

project. We could have

meant song outlasts poetry.

THYME SUITES

1

They will bring the singer to the bungalow
past the caution tape, the inviolable red trees

in the town square where we can find
crisp food from the country, and those who

wear Blake's arrows lounge on the steps, hearing
stories of an herbalist in stages, having been

trapped in their otherness a while, or in
a plan or the help or an idea,

their methods for observing interiors like looking
over the edge of a star's rim where

inside the spirit world there's a scrannel moan
or in the spirit origins an alternating beauty—

2

Three times the ringmasters tell you to jump;
you didn't like their spinning cycle, did you.

They've gone north with their charts and disappearing
brides to drill for fuel in the tundra.

A horizon lifts when you breathe, a cloud
tilts through the brutal perpendicular; there's a void

halo in the wedding planet. When will it stop
raining, do you think. Rope and candle. You work

like a phrase among phrases, mostly shadow;
threads between phenomena pull light from gravity—

3

If the net of the universe is fixed,
Indra's net is a *shigra* of beads. Rusty

trees were stuck to twin suns all winter; now
the tricolored mask faces back into eternity

and we're out here to avoid being sold
something else with the leftover seeds preparing to

jump except the gravid ones who thought
a garden was a thought; there's a stubble

in the fields again, Tuesday glitter on our

heroine. All flames she was, then water,
then air. There you are; so it grows.

FOR ANN LAUTERBACH

REVERSIBLE WIND

Night sprinkler   fsss   fssssss   fs-s-s-s-s-s-s
Vowels dropped in the three-branched world

A backward wind tips Tahoe to the left~~

Turns bluer   (Not the right galaxy amount?)

Many drunk & sleeping columbines don't know what to do

Oh, your thief sleeps too   & your singing architect & his imitators
No readier for death than you are

You look really different   Need to check your idea

Black in the amphitheater   Red tinge in the moon-soffit

Invisible times one = the visible

Each aspen leaf a coat of arms
A toothless lineage of solitude

AIR IN THE EPIC

On the under-mothered world in crisis,

the omens agree. A *Come here*   follows for reader & hero through

the named winds as spirits are

lifted through ragged colorful o's on   butterflies called fritillaries, tortoise shells &

blues till their vacation settles under

the vein of an aspen leaf   like a compass needle stopped in

an avalanche. The students are moving.

You look outside the classroom where   construction trucks find little Troys. Dust

rises: part pagan, part looping. Try

to describe the world, you tell   them—but what is a description?

For centuries people carried the epic

inside themselves. (Past the old weather   stripping, a breeze is making some

6th-vowel sounds *yyyyyy* that will side

with you on the subject of syntax   as into the word *wind* they

go. A flicker passes by: air

let out of a Corvette tire.)   Side stories leaked into the epic,

told by its lover, the world.

The line structure changed. Voices grew   to the right of all that.

The epic is carried into school

then to scooped-out chairs. Scratchy holes in acoustic tiles pull *whwhoo--* from

paperbacks. There's a type of thought

between trance & logic where teachers   rest & the mistake you make

when you're tired is not breathing.

The class is shuffling, something an   island drink might cure or a

citrus goddess. They were mostly raised

in tanklike SUVs called Caravan or   Quest; winds rarely visited them. Their

president says global warming doesn't exist.

Some winds seem warmer here. Seme.   Warriors are extra light, perhaps from

ponies galloping across the plains.

Iphigenia waits for winds to start.

Winds stowed in goatskins were meant   to be released by wise men:
gusts & siroccos, chinooks, hamsins, whooshes,
blisses, katabatics, Santa Anas, & foehns.   Egyptian birds were thought to be
impregnated by winds. The Chinese god
of wind has a red-&-blue cap   like a Red Sox fan. Students
dislike even thinking about Agamemnon. You
love the human species when you   see them, even when they load
their backpacks early & check the
tiny screens embedded in their phones.   A ponytail holder switches with light,
beguiled. Iphigenia waits for the good.
Calphas & her father have mistaken the   forms of air: Zephyr, Boreas, Eurus
the grouchy east breeze & Notos
bringer of rains. Maybe she can   see bones in the butterfly wings
before they invent the X-ray. Her
father could have removed the sails   & rowed to Troy. Nothing makes
sense in war, you say. Throw
away the hunger & the war's   all gone. There's a section between
the between of joy & terror
where the sailors know they shouldn't   open the sack of winds. It
gives the gods more credit. An
oracle is just another nature. There's   a space between the two beeps
of the dump truck where the
voice can rest. Their vowels join   the names of winds in white
acoustic tiles. A rabbit flies across
the field with Zephyr right behind.   Wind comes when warm air descends.
The imagined comes from the imagined.

[—Dimension raced through action's air collection;
            love crossed limit . . . Wasn't sure
                        (among "proved" infinities) if what we
            heard were birds outside the hospital
            or climbs in her monitor—]

NEAR STATIONS

Some of the living

were known to you

in aspects where lidlessly

their future would pass

into the amber sections

of a train, bearing

a feeling underneath emotion

of hope next to

need or chrome. From

the nets of factories,

under a window's zion

or the penny auras

on an amsel's back,

their footsteps, lawless but

ethical. Beside them, a

creature called *seven sleep*

eats grass; an excluded

middle sustains itself; chestnut

blossoms fall diagonally between

history and an endish

time. Crumble, horror; a

thought star, having thrown

throne thrown itself down

swallows the minus sign—

GREEN PANTS & A BAMBOO FLUTE

Oaks tear up the storm floor
Nothing left to warn
The poisoned rat has poisoned the owl
The striped air of the state is choked
With pointed salty star materials
They've cut the tips off dollar bills
Chipped stars everywhere it seems like
Death planes with Daisy Chains
Bombs with cute little names
Swordfish stab the water's skin
The sea has no plot

Earlier thinkers thought of air
As a mist not a context
With each bomb the part
That was narrow shrinks
Our god passes by briefly
From another existence
With his pretty floating rib
The one they call the twelfth
The webbed arch of caravans
Frames the desert horror
The owl's eyes follow them
On this side of the pale

One night in my vision place
Our future cars were buried
Today we drive a buried car
And turn like a three-part song
Electricity wants not to be anymore
Or to be darktricity
The brain is an atmosphere of rooms
A situation that needs a future
Where an *us* presides next to an *it*
Now the dooms'-whim-bride's-trace
Fog doubles as a shroud

If the flute cannot be found
Its breath is still in you
Making an *at* sign of sex or grain
What was it thinking of
The catkins look so like grenades
Maybe the particle spirits
Will spin in the @ of each address
Knock the wheel of fate from its orbit
Racc to a curled-up
Solomon's sleep in the clock's
Ring moist with air

The lord is its shepherd and i

am its color captive

its color color color captive

in the tree that

has no
inside

THE VALUE OF EMPTY PROTEST

Longing declined;
whatever had been charged with it,

what curls, what
octave flowers
angered the voice ramp

which for a while called
from their gray-rim signs
Come back to the stamped
lawn as people cheered,

wearing an abyss
for the whorled
capitol, threads dangling

from their placards,
from misery of capital, known

as a crowd
in the crowd and
they would lose again,

as a wheel loses,
taste, past,
skies reptilian and vast,

nothing to sell but being
sold, mute hands clapping at the
why of whys—

DOPPLER EFFECT IN DIAGRAM THREE

Waves past the meadow, *meu viajante*
The summer was almost straight
From cities from countries
It had straight-smelling shirts
Parentheses from the hawk a day sound
Only borders in its mouth
Almost no weather from its travels
The heat sing-ing-ing
A series of syllables not yet delivered
Families just beginning to gather
Or double gather like curtains
So much not enough you said
A hope inflected from the east
Something at rest about the waves not then
Someone swell to be remembered
In the theories of the address
Blue & the palindrome of a wave
Moving against the rest

The Earth's axis has been set aflame
The harlequin picks his teeth with a matchstick
It was called life in those decades
Dragonflies attached one per stalk
Like a music staff turned sideways
Papermill Creek before the death of paper
Incandescence is its own defense you said
Periodicity of a fear moving
Off from the too-bright years
A bike in the car its spokes turning
Click-click past goats & ravens

It's up to sounds like this to descend in size
To express surprise or terror
How does air feel with waves inside it
Does it feel more
With the radio on
How do airwaves get through all the numbers
& how does the ((((((((do it

In the model an observer stands on
The platform & we grow to love him
He is wild & is thinking of nothing
Let us call all of this observer A
There is a row of bending sounds
As the trouble curves rightward
Mr. Doppler is in heaven by now
A slim hush as the fat springs click
The men in burgundy shorts roll
The luggage carts away
People think they are you but they are not
You are you & no one & everything
The oscillating quality of dusk clashes with
What is universal just as the vowels
In a person's name clash with his handwriting
How lovely we seem as the passenger pulls away
With an identity among the abstracted
Pale diners who eat behind the cellophane

But in fact he is lost to us
As the page turner at a recital is lost
Or one who speaks of the Irish solution
Or names the roses Peace or Sally
When it starts being unbearable
Time won't pierce air with its skinny death feet

In the pulling away life is continuous
The worry hyphens inside the molecule
The sentence or the train passing
As it holds out its skirts of sound
The sentence has started its journey
But has no idea for its mystic demise
It rides in the firebox to the cave
Looking out at pines their raw huts
Bearing its constant falling
Over the laughter in the night pool of those
Who have not stopped & may not, ever

STUDY OF AIR IN TRIANGLES

Not till dawn becomes a volunteer
Will we know how it was inside this world;

Outside our café: unicyclists with knives, & translators;

When I saw the world's triangles, some letters came:

First a Y then N & especially A.

By dusk they had settled
In the voices of a nest
Where eaves spread evening around;

A robin had been feeding her isosceles-headed babies,
Their brief don't-let-me cries aflutter;

She carried out the bits of waste
Over the chamberous meadow's yellow,

Then their beaks would sink quietly down . . .

Could these birds be subject to a geometry
Based on the mystical three points of nature?

Perhaps the middle of the triangle is *mind*,
& the points are *word, world, & weather,*

Or one of the points is *mind*
& *word* is the middle —
That sort of thing.

These days, a poem comes
In an opinion which is energy
Sufficiently touching air,

Lines mostly said as not-unsayable —

WIND TREATIES

Between church bells

I held its breath:

air coming from half-states

it has visited where

dread meets ecstasy's skid-mark.

Allow us, mighty and

bruised oxygen. And I

imagined a black square

made of ariadne-thread

around the great city,

winds coming from corners

such that talking would

never cease. Talking should

never cease, heads bent

over documents allowing distinction

or zhivagoing solitudes, stitches

at the edges of

dignity. Decades of give-it-away

while these winds worked.

Lamps flickering in the

stable districts. Symbolic weight

being added to bodies

walking in ordinary courtship

outfits, in a park.

ALTAMONT PASS

Outside the white spectacle
Of the mind's blindness
In the black before last
Of the unplanned towns
Past the summer barbecue kickoff
Near the whiff of lemons
Where they had stopped moaning
Where the spinning boy's comrades
Joined the working force
The breeze turns and turns
Back of power's face or
Should that be fate, *o meu vento*

Have you seen the monarchs
They left their stripes
Wind revises them as ravens
Gnostics in recovery
Their weightlessness a source
Of autumn in the outskirts
The sun a champagne glass
Near the whiff of lemons
The air is not an error
The cattle graze crookedly
And the baby race cars
Are in flames, *mon flaneur*

We've been having a little trouble
With our cheekbones
Yellow keeps getting into them
Disguised as echo

The villages we built
Are what can't be spoken
Our lover would be a sparrower
And we his bright sparrow
The orchard-keeper looks around
Coyote cries burn knowledge
More about that later wear wings
On the inside, *mein wind Geist*

Windmills face all ways
Some *thrives* flying around
Serene mall kids wander
The ATM is jammed
Wind will rend the suburbs
With information seeking nature
We put the tractate on the table
And we his bright sparrow
Experience is peri-everything
Then thought then poetry
Silence is also everything
The silence part poetry, LW

An "i" is a suburb of it
i sat on the hill
To contact the spirit world
They do what they want
And also use geometry
Their style is post-anonymous
Pollen disguised as echo
The goats have been sacrificed
To minotaur manifestoes
Aspects of the broken fan
Like Horace's *philyra*
Circle the worlds, *il viento mio*

There's a little shudder
At the end of seeing
You blink and that's it
Have memory on us winds
The ministers of consequence
Make mostly demands
We read the printouts
On glowing tablets of azurite
Design for a quatrefoil
Syllables talk like bees
They do what they want
One per blossom and breath

[—matter chose consequence: my breath had
sent *prayer* out, (its "*y*" 2/3
of a triangle) & while he
        died, some flecked
        mushrooms appeared on
                Ashby lawns: bits of packing material]

6 COMPONENTS FROM ARISTOTLE

PLOT

End of the Cold War, some air had been forgotten and was safe.

The submarine Kursk, its night full of embalmed men used by the state—

The report in Russian translated as: *The submarine wrecked in a point 69040′N 37035′E and lied on oozy & sand ground on depth of 108 m with heel 25 degrees on port side and down 5–7 degrees by the bow. As time goes by, the submarine became covered more and more by slurry. Her heel increased for some time but stop now. The reactor is in the suppressed state. Temperature of water on depth of 100 m –3–4 degrees of Celsius, on a surface –7–8 degrees. There are many versions were discussed, including fabulous.*

Having no place to stand. The men, having no place to stand, having been disappointed by the desired presence,

crowded forward, those who never touched the control panel—

CHARACTER

A captain had been sent down but was not
returning.

The men are more of a Dido. Their hope has only one ship that keeps getting lost over and over. Vertical says to horizontal, *I can, again.* In the medium wave

the unconscious
has no breath.

In the storm they're lowering the ladder. Weather was in control as a list. In the Barents Sea they are lowering the ladder. Others called out.

After the explosion, a type of consciousness that had forgotten itself; a million beneaths, perfecting the weapon that makes no mistakes—

the place power can't know about.

THOUGHT

With two lines of thought, the mind is an angle. One line is missing: the world, eaten. They stand in back of the ship. They have grown into one. I have grown into one thinking about them. We come into this world pure, a configuration of the lack of air. We breathe the blurry *'s. We recover.

In that place indifferent to reality a type of platonic oxygen, between space itself—

why let it go. Private Dido. She's the plot, the men; the ship gets lost over and over.

DICTION

Every word from them was not inevitable. The men wait; looking up they spot the blurry *'s. The Cold War meant what it meant to be an American and not save Russians. Children practiced crouching under their desks. Kursk keeps writing all the I's throughout the years: I everyone, I universe. I kept writing the title "The Wreck of the Deutschland" in my notebook that summer and added: "but without god." How does one write when the laws that limit power have failed. Corporate with the celestial. My life in a tangle at that time. Hopkins a bit of a Dido, pretty much a burning
magpie
nun.

MELODY

Such a silly word. That point in creation when everything is worse and what you were afraid of happening happened.

A warm storm started. Wanting a word
with them.

beside
under
above
between

Governments phoned them. Could phone them. Cables sang to them. *Seemed* to sang to them. Ordinary men, as nuns for Hopkins are ordinary. Once on the shore might be sung to. Burned.

Assumed someone would rescue them, exchanging their fate for happens
to be born.

SPECTACLE

What does Aristotle mean by the sixth element? We use it for capitalism, circuses, weathers. Can we remake elements. I thought about the men in the submarine for years, their words made of non-air, all governments failing them into news then putting a tube of silence

down. The need to make form. We talked of this in class—how form can't be an error. The submarine as a tube of air meant nothing to them,

it breathed
in each

ocean on
Earth.

In the present conflict each fire equals re-used air from the Cold War. Tube of
silence

and there is
still a silence under
                        that—

WHITE FIR DESCRIPTION

—14 cones at the top with meso-tight rings of fitted pods, boy bronzes rising
  somewhat

—The usual turkey-foot top but with toes splayed 43°, 47°, 49°

—At no place does the sun show through with more politeness than in 8-inch
  rhombuses criss-crossed with daggerdowns, & the "wrestle" "with
  my heart" side

—Each needle an inch-and-a-half long more profuse toward manzanita
  than near Meeks Bay, more profane toward sound of scrub jay stopping
  then doubling

—Changeoid quiver-cripple wind starts up & lets you record: how often you
  fought a fear, half-panic laced with ennui as

—Blond oxygen hovers over the tree, in the direness of safety—an ethics that
  would *want* to want the other to get better

STATUELESS ARCHITECTURE

I passed through nature

into the next. Children

running in unsupervised shadows.

Last century's fountains learning

not to lie. Risk

to identify with only

one element since one

will die but in

the summer air around

each thought, something is

built and avoided. You

go through an arch

and aren't the arch,

just infinity of form,

curve's curve of becoming,

a phrase tracking it

to future's celadon relief.

As others dressed as

others we were supposed

to meet. Citizens walked

here without disappointment, seeing

no statue or palace

with eleven axes, patient

in the mindless heat—

THE CORPORATE NUMBER RESCUE ALBUM

ENRON EXECUTIVES TAKE THE 5TH

In the Senate, squareheadeder men than yesterday
call on the number 5
for help,
on law, the perfect length

which feels its fear being used up;

as the executives take the 5th, the oxygen
in the cup of the 5
gets formal, crisp,
to support the *tilllllt* when the number
turns on its

back—] or > —before
being hooked to the verge ledge
of the planet; the 5
fears being next

to their zeroes, their one-inflected

zeroes' face masks,
all air zeroes,
zeroes choked,
choked air, all choked air zeroes
as if from belted

slugs circling,
choking round, choked round
the glittering
waist of the world—

CONFUSED 3'S

Faint confused 3's   dialed from mobiles
        Searching for signals   from hire hovels

3's from hire hovels   airport users

Stock rubble   NASDAQ making info bubble

Crookened stubble   George's W   George's III

U-Bahn girls'   hard-on-sized cell phones
        Dialed 3's   snagged   in nylon   air

Invisibly 3's   =   half-hearts sideways

God used 3's   tons of them

Walter B *liebened* Gretel   poor 3-some helium
        Face-down mystic   *Fraulein bitte fraulein* please

Rehearten   3's for no   seized-on   power

SEPARATE 7 WITH ITS BAR
OF PERSONAL FREEDOM

In 1976   we never met   I read
Nerves   which lived   & now   from a

Huge non-   splashy north   the inner scissors

Of / \ / \ a junco couple   befriend & clip
Atonal   irradiating cloth   of   lifesized spring

Oak wants   its bark back   a think-stopping

Drink   While   you are   invisible please rescue
Oxygen   why don't you   List in   it

Sailor   Even   dry   its hands in prose

FOR JOHN WIENERS

ETHICAL 6

Now with our tiny tinny song
It's time   to rescue   #6

Which is done   by calling   Pythagoras

Problem is   hiding it   from   Halliburton

Well   Make 6   the radical unknown

Dedicated to the   Universal analog   upside-down
Only Curlier   Call that 6th-grade boy

With his   homemade crying   Find a

Scrunch-6ish   Berkeley snail   Ethics lines
Existence   Its   nautilus air   not tricked

Thus saving   Rivers   robertduncan   shaman 6

Its   chambers   writhing   its barrel   filled

THE *E* IN *BEING*

(—*eeee* in a mountain meadow:
killdeer? middle of: breathless of
pale lands:
no style, *eeee*'s of
glacier, bristled past white:

harvest of:
doomed unsayable
letters in even
eyes of aspens, spiked
knots, could
not have been triangular:

your voice grown
raggedy thoughtful, flying
in crimped
spaces, layers
heard into straps
of ground,

shouldered letters might suffer
as you did, seacipher
then a good
second to you, mixed;
were you edged
of night, frate

among Earth &
other favorites, edged
in why, & couldn't

alive? buried in
reeds, discovered hollowish
in atmospheres,

middle of syllable's
casing, note key, &
were you not content,
trooped with
eternity till
eternity switched sides: crater

of *yes*, having been brightly
caged, a
coax tree at beginning
of end, crater of
yeses, &
hadn't you been twice

rescued this hour,
end of middle, middle of
apprentice
& ballast
as the nothing wheeled?)

[~ as the too-bright coffin handles were
set down: a slight   breeze   where
        arch is delayed—cirrus clouds in
                Olema trees   above her cheer;   passerine
birds stayed . . .   How did wind feel,
brightness betrayed, entering   such social ground?]

ON CARMERSTRASSE

Beneath balustrades selected against

your going, a breezened

day anticipates a hope;

then the walk into

each word is infinite

and navigates the stumble.

under the porticoes at

childhood's edge where half-said

sentences assemble in bombed

or not bombed corners

you, hurrying back to

the poem near a

compound diplomat's swanlet canal's

day from a bottle

where bears hold hands:

whether or not you

do the work involves

negotiating with the drama

of class shadow. Now

a trance has been

cast over the world,

but which? From a

chained bench, the soul

turns to its example.

FOR JOACHIM SARTORIUS

.

NINE UNTITLED EPYLLIONS

Something about breathing
The air inside a war

As they approached the capital
We couldn't see what was breathing from the back
Calves' horns a-swizzle
Ten thousand years of instruments
Decent amounts of free forevers

Horizons emphatically lifted in them

As they approached the place
The size of B

Saw the exhalation of an "enemy"
Breath being thought of
It had a kind of lining in it

You believed in the tuneless yes
Believed in the O very tunelessness
As they approached the capital
With dusty signs and needs

All blendy breathing
There
There is

A river that would drink water
An earth that would walk dirt
A fire that would singe flame
In that air

I made a winged

creature, and when they

bring it through each

desert on a flag

of bar codes and minus signs

in poverty of fact

through their present freedom,

it is then my

sweet-beaked creature stands for

nothing; it is then

in the frail startfulness

the creature dreams its

situations though the O

blood river it cannot

cross nor the *y*

in abyss, sleeps for

the them whose helmets

lost their eyes in

the s/hell oil past

the nineveh tent—though,

actually it isn't dreaming

yet; you better start

the other flag, assassin

air, now, citizen syllable.

As you enter the moving aura of the epic
When they carry the torn descriptions
If they arrive at the goat
Over the centuries you've often thought

When you enter the colorless
Center of the epic
If they sideways a harp
After the inlaid griffin
Into a courtyard of foam and mint

It is then a single air will spin the epic
Suffering of a little epic

When a goat voice twirls a word on its side
For instance their beige word *freedom*
If ladies and gentlemen the precedent
Of the united sales
When they take down the barricades

Over the centuries you've often wished
There was nothing
There is something

Maimed heart walled city
A hero in the scalene wind
Scrapes some breath off his shoes

In the colorful moving center of the epic
You've often thought

I am a seamstress.

I have no country.

So when I count

our dying hero's breaths

as stitches carrying Trotsky

south, it seems cloth

is a state though

every century changes what

cloth is. Now you

might enter: what kind

of cloth is your

soul, do you think.

This world's violent, comforting

machine has made it

general. The lost one

is everywhere; you won't

recover him. Hero, machine—

vowels color things but

only you provide distinction:

the curved dove back

and fourth vowel bells—

any sounds, actually—which

because they are uneven

call you from suffering—

So things were known in the uprisings;
numbers arranged in dots,
in tiny patterns, according to Pythagoras;
fire was pulled from the seem of the leaf
where death the boomerang
moth had fed—;

to the you born a thousand times,
you too tired to punctuate,
it had been pointed out,
had been implied repeatedly,

read as the L between word and world,
red between the rue and the bed:

for government, this: a mouse straddles the lion.

for government, this: in a patch of sun.

Be what
orange? Be what
orange? this window: your cerecloth;
the barricade, c'est more.

A glass mosquito has traveled eons to get here.
Come in little glass boy with your cool red zipper then

enter the flock:

help night help help help help help—!
many helps later, or less, or more:

the square has been cleared of stragglers—

After their freedom had

started I fled for

the flatness I felt

had no horizon then:

their global killed people

it would never see;

a dove with Nike

checkmarks on its wings

flies from 16th-century scenes

where we're making glass

& flax in the countryside::

ferrule of plows::: bronze

backgrounds for new towns—;

do you feel this

we in you sometimes?

I hope that you

do. Haunted by the

need to work, blinded

by cloth, I take

my needle through gates

of ivory and gates

of horn, I sew,

I push the little

bright thing on through—

Through rooms in tents
Writing insane documents
Better was a being later
They go and they went
And didn't they really
Did they blur did they talk
Your town past descriptions of it

Embedded with Bechtel McDonald's
With Daddy War- or Starbucks' floating voice
Over e-e-e-each
Exploded body into third forever
News briefs with short particulars

You of driving dust
They carry what you own
Anthems make you mute
The soul is a construct writes the palimpsest
Ten thousand souls lost writes the pencil

You of star powder
Asleep in your wagon
By the ruined wall
You are called to phalansteries and guns
With angstroms of hope and violence you are
Called to come after in your
After you are called

Beside estival smelt fields,

ilex woods, by bone

mist threading knights' mail,

hesp, fatigue, brought to

jebel, desert, by tank,

horse, through a million

wars, my needle means

nothing to the State.

Generals bring the banners

it sewed, it sewed

stars, signs, sickles, winged

creatures; my needle leans

through cloth shroud breath,

hears with its eye

of can't decide. Warped

shroud flag's white red

white white white white

thread. Near madhouses, mills,

towns spring up; wrapped

soldiers are sewn. The

needle improvises shown each

wideless war betweens. It

does the dead betweens.

It goes the gauntlet.

In the malls new babies sleep beside
dry fountains.
The tiles predict the future like Aeneas's shield.
Blankets from many invaded countries cover the babies with brief
and darling pales.
The war is forget forgot forgotten.
Siblings run wildly around.

      The mall is a square with bumps like a small epic.
      Through vents, winds swirl:
      1) a sort of sweet lite rock 2) faded popcorn
      3) infinity 4) a breezy o in the word *world*.

There is no ego. It passes
through as residue of crowd
or tone.
Holiday t-shirt gold trumpets hang low.
Past narcotic bells in the suburbs, loose mists (*loosatic*
is the word
needed here but Microsoft
has rejected it) make brain-shaped clouds.

The holes where the children sleep
are to be your work: what what
what what what what
why. It was
a judgeless
dream, including the very day it liked to provide.

Two

Wind. What do we know about it? Where is it from? Where is it going? Some love it, it's gentle with them—carries coolness on hot days, fuels the cold night's fire. Others hate it, it ruins their hair, its howl causes terror. It's everywhere and in everything, with everyone and with no one . . . I want to be everywhere and with everyone, but at the same time love solitude. I don't understand myself, let alone anyone else; it's difficult to think of yourself as wind, it's a struggle with the irreparable and reveling in carelessness. It's a thousand "why's?" It's a million wishes and aspirations. A lover called me "Wind." From that moment I knew my name. When you understand your true name, it gets easier—

SASHA BELYAEVA

draw it out   glistening

into the fabric of intentions

another body my body is

ROBERT DUNCAN

[& thrived to see *obligation*

        as mild reward: even,

        a "spillage" of suffering   ]

YOUR FATE

Waiting for the tech support person
to come back, rereading the epic—
actually, the translator's notes; strange to
start liking the on-hold music (Here's
a section where chaotic motion, interims
of wandering, invisible orders meet twisted
blue marginalia from school, doodles, what
wasn't done behind a page giving
way to cricket operas—ch-chch—&
eucalyptus residue under various protests in
spring; you could find a golden
twig, go sexily to hell, play
music below; some epics are interchangeable;
others agree to the maenads, not
you; a Sybil sings in smoggy
crags behind the hill; harps might
help, units of twelve; chance rides
at your back on his bike
but fate rides only in reverse)
tech support hasn't returned yet but
he will (there's a patient tap
tap tapping in the text; an
inviolable tree where stars pass;
stars passed; stars pierced you—

ECHO 858

1

Attempting to describe paint dear
someone arrives at the left

and says *Hello Nice Echo.*

New clove oil keeps
a green cliff

rivery but how long

will the shininess survive? ——

Long enough to try by itself
which is totally fine because

I would like to record

a feeling that isn't there.

2

A little rip in the thought
violence;

paint is just another kind of victim.

In the play between constriction and

destruction
something is risked among the agate clothes;

we hear him talking through
the stroke~~

the particles have come through uncritically but

really, it is Marx coming through like

spirits of the Baader-Meinhof
who they say "hanged themselves."

3

I looked below

the air behind the paintings.

It was trying to do something
unsystematic with our angel till

there was nothing to keep except

chance;

I made my eyes pointy to look at air in
corners,

the strong vertical inside that sucks itself
down in the gesture of

a tear, then a miracle revealed a
blue lake.

4

To have an argument
with existence you can wait

till it says something then
say nothing. With the speed

inside set to your childhood

a fleck of grandfather's barn comes through the nicely
drying doves,--

so many more colors than the one
you're obsessed with. The kir

of a candy czar we once knew—

was a rose buried in there too?

your hope for it is yes.

5

With the fire that has gathered in me

I put my head to the wall to see the gargoyle
pushing
from the back of the painting—it loves and chokes the painting—

but no use; details are spurs that hurt us
when we try to mount extra beauty. The artist

has proceeded with not one
color but

twins which is why art historians sound stoned.

N sitting on the floor under #8 holding her bandage up

for here, we're little divers
giving Oz value to hiding behind the curtain~~

6

Great paint resists the character. You
know this.
If you tilt your head sideways the

smoothness

feels

something. It does not tell you till the magic

probes. The air tripling and crippling,

D holds our hand as
we nearly skip the ladder up to air

that rises behind the east
where bombing is. Great bird perched in

the limb/o where contradiction kills time.

7

To escape
the war we watched a color
field with its line

emphatically drawn in a daily

way;

our love had dreamed and faced
the bedspread

from a wide-wing chair;

what has never not
existed grows horizons

in it. Why bother trying to

trap it with description.

8

You shouldn't ever say
you'll give up art. Why did you say that? Take it back.

The interesting length is always death

but paint and ink
resist no matter

what

stages of furious alarm are
set;

the combed paint takes a line

from Hamlet—a point in fact
that hesitates. How strange to give up wanting. Life's

action amazes you.

MANZANITA DESCRIPTION

—Of the abstract green-&-a-half leaves, 38 have no other color than
    nephew yellow

—A low u————~————hollow from behind Sierra granite more than
    16 times the size of fair leaf ovals to forget the bombing

—Grainy brain clouds on top of the capillary silkish i-can't-wait-to-be-
    them clouds toward the lake

—More graywood party holding up the livelier balance of succulent leaves,
    sub-holly serrations & scallops nimbly choosing sun

—Scrub jay comes along & masters the chee-chee, 6 serene dragonflies,
    competing jays flown by every very hour

—Redwood only 2/3 facing the downhill slope, my mother's narrow shapely
    summon bell rang just that color

I   will   lift   up   mine   blindfold

down   round   eyes   unto the   hills

& the   swallow flew across   six fields

from   whence cometh mine   for we

were   both   (no we were all)

temptation's types

CLOUDS NEAR SAN LEANDRO

I

The crack in social justice widened;
we saw the sparkle shelf below;

there had been some fragile delays
in back of the noetic cities,

berries on the blood ledge, sun-
lords with their seeds of steel,

snakes winding in the hungry age.
In the middle of our life

the dark woods had been clear-cut;
furies changed to quires of orange,

in spring, pelicans seen flying hillward,
their beaks like cut-up credit cards.

II

In the middle of your life
you cast aside the brittle flame;

the doctor took some cancer off,
pain ceased to be an organizer.

Hadn't you preferred Nefertiti's blank left

eye to the rest? shape of
seeds the blue jays love, white

as the dream-egg heart of a
6 the courtier used for calling

other courtiers with his thumb—

III

We're done with the old ironies,
is the thing of it. Some

foolish soul has sold his entire
Liz Phair collection back to Amoeba;

Used jewel cases seem almost tender,
smothered-to-smithereens-type plastic like

the mythic selves in Nietzsche, comet
making a comeback, the endless sheen—

IV

So shake off the iron shoes
of fame and image and sing

near the dumb branch. Or enter
the pond where the angles swam.

Aren't there visions involving everything?
Some animals are warm in paradise;

your little alchemical salamander *taricha tarosa*,
fresh from the being cycles, stumbles

over rocks in its lyric outfit—

::: AN ODDNESS :::

A scent   rather quietly   loves

the library.   Readers   look up: a

life of paper   inside   the great

Life: scent of greenly   ravished civilization--

dream of inspiration   freed.   When a

book is   lifted   from horizon's steel

that mystery   object   spreads   an oddness

each call number   a timeling of

yellow math,   its curve   leftover from

epic.   The mind   had no   periphery

for meaning,   the several phoenician,   sailing

sideways   through vowels   of the dead.

::: SILENT READING :::

Thought   makes tablets   Ruins   cry stone

Pounded reeds Cracked bone prophecies Home's

cuneiform   One soonday   Caesar burns scrolls

vellum vines   riddles   Thought becomes stylish

Saved by syntax   Augustine loves Alypius

October   the birdbacked   Joy marries doubt

in a font   Thenceforth   some shall

read noiselessly   seated   Some shall curl

eyes to slightly   mix air   &

script   forefinger to lips   To hold

halfway   letters from visible   or with

To have no cause   but breath

::: A NEXTOPIA :::

Past modernisms,   a library   smells spicy,

   spicy and tuneful—   a treble clef

on its side.   Readers touch   each

   book's   crowded energies   with wind-whirled

   fingers,   a personal   blond   number   on

its spine.   Sleeves brush   complete works

   by accident: mothers,   a prowl   isaiah,

a gyroscope   girl with two   kinds-of-gone—

   When paper lived   in the Radiance

   Forest,   stored blindfold   gray;   sleeps nicely

now—   after sunlight   training   (invited measure)

   as if   a shadow   sat down —

Thoughts   are odd   Even   normal thoughts

   Nature   within nature Vowels where sex-

   cries   recover   An oddness   made your

book   a world   The whisper   furnace

   blows bent   crackly motes   through readers'

delft   blue auras   Were   you   afraid

your   book would vanish   Thought   kabbalahs

it   Dust motes   land   immaturely from

   joy   or have to   Race   to

   perform   as a dying   man's twin

breaths   might sound like turning   same

   or   added   pages   on the inside

An aura   survives the discipline of

a flower, goes back to the

fertile   Tree, knowing   you are aware:

around each   letter of a book

trial colors   of a heart. In

terror   or trusted mildness   the Tree

prepared.   Readers at praxis screens   move

numbers   to a noon   alliance with

searchers: the velcro kafka,   some   bacchae,

an ask-to-be-shown. Time is   inspiration

for your readers. In free   oxygen

books lean rightward;   some pleasure moan--

::: DUST ACOLYTES :::

Who   has come?   What ironfoot   iliad

   girl approaches   the PS's, her weathers

      locked   in gray flame?   A steep

scent   sends energy back   through the

fate myth.   Readers walk   mazedly carrying

   your book--   Did you   love paper

more than people?   Perhaps its healing

     colors wooed you: calendula, filter beacon

yellow on its spine, an asterisk

falling   from the owl's eyes.   A

   duality   has been renounced. Then paper

the pain sail   turned   to harbor--

Air in the   stretched *therefore* part

of the library   smells gnostic like the

back of a mask.   Glue from

meal & bone   cooked in iron

pots.   In epics,   this always happens:

mixtures of research   & rural, searchful

frass &   some might say   used

god parts.   So much stubborn air

escapes   the canon. A dream makes

its own lining.   Sweet artaud dust

flies   through decades, lands   where a

sprawl isaiah   sleeps in an armchair~~

Readers are crying   in the HF's;

the epoch of paper   loses breath:

graphs & maps,   prone algebra swiggles;

knowledge is lonely   since   meaning left.

A seaquake   dire & sleety   marx

boy passes   holding your book   (might

pass   might hold)   its fabric   shipped

tariffless   by cypher code.   Old Blake

sleeps upside down   in the radiance

forrest   six aisles hence   then anti-sleeps,

a bunchy   brown aura   around his

head   while dust   contrives   the paradox‑‑

What   is thought   Is it breath

Were you breath   Was paper   skin

Turns out   there *are* bugs   that

     eat book glue   birth slash death

of knowledge   in their bodies   Readers

rest on backpacks   An isis in

corduroy   Crimson kierkegaard   on her lap

   Dust motes   leap   through brass rings

    of library   light   How each one

feels   The smallest ring   is everything

   The middle ring   is number glory

The largest ring is   in between

::: **RESTLESS AURAS** :::

The idea   of auras   being uneven

Gleam starts crowding   the readers' eyes

   A local spinning   round each consonant

Talking ceases in it   Did you

     not   also   swerve to avoid   hubcaps

from a masterpiece   Tired readers use

   invisibilities   Aporias   Fast purple

noise   above them as   they pack

their laptops   Unchecked-out books   on

   low tables   keep   the fragrance

of masks   Some haptic   call numbers

spin on fabric   Prove back Pythagoras

::: **DUST DIALECTICAL** :::

Learning to see   extra light over

heads   of readers   when sitting   using

blur   techniques.   Late auras are being

swept   out.   In the library   stacks,

a flexidrama: these   yellow rooms   excite

the sun.   Dust comes from   galaxies,

each mote   bent   at the waist

like a poetry translator,   slight   train-

trace   of sleeper breath, horizon   hair

a flame   of doubt.   In evening

outside,   streaked doves   & semaphores   pull

smiles   from the queen   of clouds~~

::: EPOCH OF DUST :::

Thought has life   Day makes   samples

Library   lamps   gold outly   like a

prom   going dim   & dust sails

into   the public sphere   *I should*

not mind   a mote might   say

An aisle away   the squeak   of

running shoes   Squeak thump   Your page

is   almost chosen   There's a fading

threshold   at the edge   of seeing

Between each word   the century rests

its nothing air   Write *dust*   Write

live   Live hidden   Live hidden   here

STRING THEORY SUTRA

There are so many types of
"personal" in poetry. The "I" is

a needle some find useful, though

the thread, of course, is shadow.
In writing of experience or beauty,

a cloth emerges as if made

from a twin existence. It's July
4: air is full of mistaken

stars & the wiggly half-zeroes stripes

make when folded into fabric meant
never to touch ground ever again—

the curved cloth of Sleeping Beauty

around 1310, decades after the spinning
wheel gathered stray fibers in a

whir of spindles before the swath

of the industrial revolution, & by
1769 a thread stiff enough for

the warp of cotton fabric from

the spinning frame, the spinning jenny,
the spinning "mule" or muslin wheel,

which wasn't patented. By *its*, I

mean *our*, for we would become
what we made. String theory posits

no events when it isn't a

metaphor; donut twists in matter—10
to the minus 33 cm—its

inverted fragments like Bay Area poetry—

numbers start the world for grown-ups,
& wobbly fibers, coaxed from eternity,

are stuffed into stems of dates

like today so the way people
are proud of their flag can

enter the pipes of a 4.

Blithe astonishment in the holiday music
over the picnickers: a man waves

from his spandex biking outfit, cloth

that both has & hasn't lost
its nature. Unexpected folds are part

of form where our park is

kissed by eucalyptus insect noises ^^z-
z-~> *crr*, making that for you.

Flag cloth has this singing quality.

Airline pilots wear wool blend flag
ties from Target to protect their

hearts. Women, making weavings of

unicorns in castles, hummed as they sewed
spiral horns with thread so real
by figures in beyond-type garments so
they could ask how to live.
Flying shuttles, 1733, made weaving like
experience, full of terrible accidents &
were made in countries we bombed
in the last war. By *we*
means *the poem.* By *it* I
mean meanings which hang tatters of
the druid oak with skinny linguistic
branches, Indo-European roots & the
came to me in a dream
beyond time: *love, we are your*
with stereo eyes spoke over my
head. I am a seamstress for
hear. It puts its head on
our laps. Fibers, beauty at a
industry of thought. Threads inspired this
textile picnic: the satin ponytail holder,
saris, threads of the basketball jersey,
turbans, leis over pink shorts, sports
—he's like Chekhov, an atheist believer
in what's here—that sometimes, sitting
"God bless you." It seems to
help somewhat. They don't know what
I mean the *internet.* Turns out
all forces are similar to gravity.
we I mean *we.* Sewed it
us-wards, with flaws between strings.
in the Planck scale. My sisters
& I worked for the missing
aren't. A paradox. There are some

it floated; such artists were visited

It's all a kind of seam.

progress. Flags for the present war

you mean *they.* By *you* it

dawn's early light in wrinkled sections of

weird particle earth spirits. A voice

shadow thread -- A little owl

the missing queen. The unicorn can't

low level, fabric styles, the cottage

the gauze pads inside Band-Aids,

bras: A young doctor told us

with his dying patients, he says,

causes delays between strings—by *they,*

We searched for meaning ceaselessly. By

It seems there is no revolution

queen: she said: be what you

revolutions: rips in matter, the bent

nots inside our fabric whirred &

barely mattered anymore. Our art
could help take vividness to people

but only if they had food.

No revolution helped the workers, ever,
very long. We worked on this

or that flag after sewing this

or that unicorn. They called Trotsky
back from Canada. Tribes were looser

than nations, nations did some good

but not so very always, &
the types of personal in art

turned & turned. Nylon parachutes in

1937. Lachesis. We shall not flag
nor fail, wrote Churchill. O knight,

tie our scarf on your neck.

There are more than two ways
to make beauty so movements end

like sutras or horizons, somewhat frayed.

Je est un autre wrote Rimbaud
the gun-runner. Over & inner &

code. The unicorn, *c'est moi.* The

rips by which the threads are
tethered to their opposites like concepts

of an art which each example

will undo. We spoke of meanings.
I, it, we, you, he, they

am, is, are sick about America.

Colors forgive flags—red as the
fireskirt of the goddess Asherah, white
as the gravity behind her eye,
blue for the horizon unbuttoned so

the next world can get through.

The "thin thread of calculable continuity"
Santayana refers to —it's not a

choice between art & life, we

know this now, but still: How
shall we live? *O shadow thread.*

After the cotton workers' lockout 1922

owners cut back sweatshop hours to
44 per week. In string theory

the slippage between string & theory

makes air seem an invented thing
& perhaps it is, skepticism mixed

with fear that since nothing has

singular purpose, we should not act.
To make reality more bearable for

some besides ourselves? There's a moment

in Southey's journal when the tomb
is opened & the glow-beast exits—
revolutionized their work—by *their* I
mean *our*—& cut costs by
continue them & if you do
help the others, don't tell. String theory
'tis of installing provisional governments.
Why was love the meaning thread.
matter what: washable rayon, airport
carpets, checked flannel smocks of nurses,
aprons with insignias or socks people
wear before/during sexual thrills after
t-shirts worn by crowds in raincoats.
Human fabric is dragged out, being
which is also joy. Einstein called mystery
of existence "the fundamental emotion."
you were everything. By *everything* I mean
everything. The unicorn puts its head
sees the blurry edge. How am
I so unreal & yet my

right when the flying shuttle has

half. So lines are cut to

posits symmetry or weight. My country

Textiles give off tiny singing no

caps, pillowcases, prom sashes, & barbecue

dark subtitled Berkeley movies next to

is sewn with terror or awe

Remember? You unraveled in childhood till

on your lap; from there it

thread is real it asks sleepily~~

SUMMER GARDEN

~~ & thus you entered

a forest of solitudes

where in this great

sense your life had

been pursued, till like

a shadow breaking off

a rising body, a

need hovered & grew.

Some lined feature of

another fate strives to

be met, sits low

& upright. Those qualities

which had been energy

or grace past pain

wove from the nerves

a nest or instinct.

Your calms are interesting.

Write to us during

this terrible government. A

universe coughs blue &

draws a twiceness from

the mitred now, while

your garden hand spells

the inexhaustible forms~~

FOR ELIZABETH ROBINSON

MARS FIELD SPEAKS TO VVEDENSKY

Now that   the nerves   are vapor,
void violates   the homesick *what*   &
winds   from the Gulf   of F

circle bodies,   little Nevsky Prospekt dancers'
fast   red cummerbunds,   isn't it odd
that syllables   still speak to words

through   endurable doubt, a Now   ceaselessly
folded in?   Weren't we   always here?
You   swept & slept.   Fires ringed

the city.   You were advised   to
stay put: basements   of leather: breath
of the unborn;   bracelets of ether.

EYES IN ASPENS

The path ascends itself.
In the grown dusk, the light is not yet bound
        to make an original vault; it does not emerge
        from corners by accident.
You are calm. Lightning somehow lasted. We were calm,
it foreshortened viewers at the lake. The patterns
hold others in.
The sun will return with extra data, dear moment, soon.

Come into the split moonbeam
which can match your mind
to the meanings they wanted. Come

to the compounds that will ignite the figure 8 over the golden
        rod, the gravel ghost.

The rocks left their bunting; three spiders drop
down: Clotho, Atropos, the third mythically forgotten.

We have replaced the garden with dew
rooms;
the river lily has been folded without objection.
You felt safe because horizon lightning made H or Z or N.

Follow us into the struck minerals,
a swallow. In a meadow
different temperatures are asked to remain what we are
wearing;
when you finally saw the lace-maker's dress, it was
precise and limitless.

ACKNOWLEDGMENTS AND NOTES

Many thanks to people who read these poems at various stages, & to editors of period-icals & anthologies in which they were published or will be published: *American Let-ters & Commentary, American Poetry Review, Atomic Poetry, Bayou, Bay Poetics (* Faux Press), *Canary, Carnet de Route* (online), *caesura, Chain, Colorado Review, Conduit, Conjunctions, Crowd, 14 Hills, Literary Imagination, Lyric Postmodernism, Mangrove, New American Writing, 1913: a journal of forms, nocturnes (re)view of the literary arts* nos. *2, 4,* & *5, Poets Against the War, Pool, Ribot, Runes, The Squaw Valley Anthology, Vix: Interarts Magazine, Volt, Washington Square Literary Journal, Watershed, Waterstone,* & *Xantippe.* Thanks to Quemadura & Wesleyan University Press for producing this book, to Gary Frost, Robert Kaufman & Doug Richstone for information, to John Lucas for images, & to Steven Barclay & Garth Bixler for the sojourn. The *Odyssey* quote is from the Robert Fagles translation. The Franz Hessel quote is translated from German by Howard Eiland & Kevin McLaughlin; it appears in *The Arcades Project* by Walter Benjamin. "They will bring the singer to the bungalow" is sometimes used by speech therapists for rehabilitating speech. "Wind Treaties" was reprinted as a broadside in honor of Tom & Val Raworth by Empyrean Press. "Throw away the hunger / And the war's all gone" is a quote from Stiff Little Fingers. The prose poem by Sasha Belyaeva, written on fabric, is translated from Russian by Len Shneyder. The quote by Robert Duncan is from "The Torn Cloth" in *Groundwork: Before the War.* "Echo 858" was part of a collaborative project in honor of Gerhard Richter; it was published in *Richter 858,* edited by David Breskin. Half-tractates: for Carol Thigpen Milosz, Helen Louise Hass, & Leonard Michaels, in memoriam. "Nine Untitled Epyllions" are dedicated to all who have suffered & died as a result of the war in Iraq.

ABOUT THE AUTHOR

Brenda Hillman lives in the Bay Area and teaches
at Saint Mary's College in Moraga, California.

_LL_ DATE DUE _W - 13_

WITHDRAWN

GAYLORD   PRINTED IN U.S.A.